WORLD WAR I

Remembering the Great War

CANADA IN WORLD WAR I

Outstanding Victories Create a Nation

GORDON CLARKE

 Crabtree Publishing Company

www.crabtreebooks.com

WORLD WAR I

Remembering
the Great War

Author: Gordon Clarke
Editor: Lynn Peppas
Proofreader: Lisa Slone, Wendy Scavuzzo
Editorial director: Kathy Middleton
Production coordinator: Shivi Sharma
Design: Margaret Amy Salter
Cover design: Ken Wright
Photo research: Nivisha Sinha, Crystal Sikkens
Maps: Contentra Technologies
Production coordinator and
Prepress technician: Katherine Berti
Print coordinator: Katherine Berti

Written, developed, and produced by
Contentra Technologies

Cover: Canadian soldiers during the Battle
of Vimy Ridge load a QF 4.5 inch
howitzer gun
Title page: Canadian soldiers from the 48th
Highlanders, 12th Infantry, and 10th Royal
leave Toronto, Canada, for training camp at
the beginning of World War I
Contents Page: German prisoners captured
during the Somme Campaign, 1916

Photo Credits:
Alamy: 6 (© Gino's Premium Images), 6 (© SOTK2011), 17 (© Bygone Collection), 20
(© PF-(wararchive), 21 (© SOTK2011)
The Bridgeman Art Library: 23 (The Hour has Struck! British First line of attack take
up position in front of their barbed-wire defences, July 1st, 1916 (litho), English
School, (20th century) / Private Collection / The Stapleton Collection), 31b
(Major (Temporary Lieutenant-Colonel) A.F. Douglas-Hamilton rallies his men
and leads them forward, thus checking the enemy's advance (litho), Ripperger,
H. (fl.1915) / Private Collection / The Stapleton Collection)
Canadian War Museum: 9b (George Metcalf Archival Collection), 16 (Beaverbrook
Collection of War Art), 25 (Beaverbrook Collection of War Art), 39 (Beaverbrook
Collection of War Art), 40t (Beaverbrook Collection of War Art), 40b (Beaver-
brook Collection of War Art), 41b (Beaverbrook Collection of War Art)
Corbis: 4 (© Bettmann), 44t , 44b (© Hulton-Deutsch Collection)
Getty Images: 5 (Hulton Archive), 6 (UIG via Getty Images), 6 (UIG via Getty Im-
ages), 9t (Hulton Archive), 10b (Archive Photos), 12 (Archive Photos), 13 (Print
Collector), 18 (UIG via Getty Images), 22 (Time & Life Pictures), 28 (UIG via
Getty Images), 33 (Popperfoto), 42 (Time & Life Pictures), 43 (Hulton Archive)
© Imperial War Museums (INS 6062): 19, 27, 29, 30
India Picture: Content Page (Heritage Images), 31t (Mary)
Library of Congress: 8 (LC-USZC4-10650), 10t (LC-DIG-ggbain-06369)
Library and Archives Canada: 26 (Department of National Defence fonds), 29
(Frank C. Wiliams collection), 36 (Department of National Defence fonds), 38
(William Rider-Rider/Department of National Defence fonds)
Shutterstock.com: 6 (admin_design;), 6 (Paul Stringer), 6 (Fotogroove), 6 (Gil C), 6
(Bildagentur Zoonar GmbH), 6 (issumbosi), 6 (Atlaspix), 6 (SurangaSL), 6 (Peter
Wemmert), 6 (Globe Turner), 6 (Julinzy), 6 (Paul Stringer)
Wikipedia: 6 (Jaume Ollé), 6, 17b
Cover: Wikimedia Commons: Library and Archives Canada
Title page: Library of Congress (LC-DIG-ggbain-16977)
Back cover: Wikimedia Commons: Library and Archives Canada (background)
Shutterstock: I. Pilon (medals); Shutterstock: IanC66 (airplane)

t=Top, b=Bottom, l=Left, r=Right

Library and Archives Canada Cataloguing in Publication

Clarke, Gordon, 1965-, author
    Canada in World War I : outstanding victories creating a nation /
Gordon Clarke.

(World War I : remembering the Great War)
Includes index.
Issued in print and electronic formats.
ISBN 978-0-7787-0327-3 (bound).--ISBN 978-0-7787-0392-1 (pbk.).--
ISBN 978-1-4271-7504-5 (pdf).--ISBN 978-1-4271-7498-7 (html)

    1. World War, 1914-1918--Canada--Juvenile literature. 2. World
War, 1914-1918--Campaigns--Juvenile literature. 3. Canada--History--
1914-1918--Juvenile literature. I. Title.

D547.C2C53 2014   j940.4'0971   C2014-903232-3
                                              C2014-903233-1

Library of Congress Cataloging-in-Publication Data

Clarke, Gordon, 1965-
 Canada in World War I : outstanding victories create a nation / Gordon Clarke.
     pages cm. -- (World War I: remembering the Great War)
 Includes index.
  ISBN 978-0-7787-0327-3 (reinforced library binding : alk. paper) -- ISBN 978-0-
7787-0392-1 (pbk. : alk. paper) -- ISBN 978-1-4271-7504-5 (electronic pdf : alk.
paper) -- ISBN 978-1-4271-7498-7 (electronic html : alk. paper)
 1. World War, 1914-1918--Canada--Juvenile literature. 2. Canada. Canadian
Army--History--World War, 1914-1918--Juvenile literature. 3. Canada. Canadian
Army. Canadian Corps--History--Juvenile literature. 4. World War, 1914-1918--
Campaigns--Juvenile literature. I. Title. II. Title: Canada in World War One.

D547.C2C553 2014
940.4'0971--dc23
                                              2014017797

Crabtree Publishing Company
www.crabtreebooks.com   1-800-387-7650

Printed in Canada/052014/MA20140505

Published in Canada
Crabtree Publishing
616 Welland Ave.
St. Catharines, Ontario
L2M 5V6

Published in the United States
Crabtree Publishing
PMB 59051
350 Fifth Avenue, 59th Floor
New York, New York 10118

Published in the United Kingdom
Crabtree Publishing
Maritime House
Basin Road North, Hove
BN41 1WR

Published in Australia
Crabtree Publishing
3 Charles Street
Coburg North
VIC, 3058

CONTENTS

ABOVE: *German prisoners captured by Allied troops at the Battle of the Somme.*

CALLED TO SERVE

World War I had numerous causes. Alliances for defense in war brought the major powers of Europe into two groups. Britain, France, and Russia formed the Allied Powers. Germany and Austria-Hungary formed the Central Powers. Other countries were drawn toward these groups as the war began. Members of the British Empire, including Canada, were pulled into the war for the Allies. Wars in the Balkans between 1912 and 1913 broke many old alliances. New alliances formed, as the smaller **Balkan** countries tried to tie themselves to larger powers. A rise in **nationalism** among all of the countries in Europe created tension. In June 1914, Archduke Franz Ferdinand, heir to the throne of Austria-Hungary, was assassinated by a Bosnian-Serb. Austria-Hungary declared war on Serbia. The chain of alliances began drawing other nations into the war.

BELOW: *Young Austrians eagerly stood in line to sign up to serve when Austria-Hungary declared war on Serbia.*

ABOVE: *A Berlin crowd listens as a German officer reads the Kaiser's order for mobilization on August 1, 1914. The following day, the German army invaded Luxembourg on its way to Belgium and France.*

Many of the major powers of Europe depended on their colonies, or the territories they controlled throughout the world. In the early 1900s, Canada governed itself. It was still a colony of Britain though. This meant that Britain determined Canada's relations with foreign powers. Most of Canada's dealings with the rest of the world came through Britain and the United States, Canada's southern neighbor.

In the years leading up to the war, Canada saw many changes. Many Canadians wanted Canada to control its own foreign relations, not be directed by Britain. Canada's connection with the United States was also growing stronger through increased trade.

The majority of Canadians had British ancestors, and many felt Canada should support Britain by joining the fight. Canadians with French ancestors did not all feel the same obligation to Britain, nor even to France. Some Canadians, both English and French, did not like the idea of Canada being dragged into European conflicts. They wanted Canada to be more independent.

As with other nations, World War I would bring many changes to Canada.

WHAT DO YOU THINK?
How did Canadians view Canada's relationship with Britain?

European Powers Before World War I

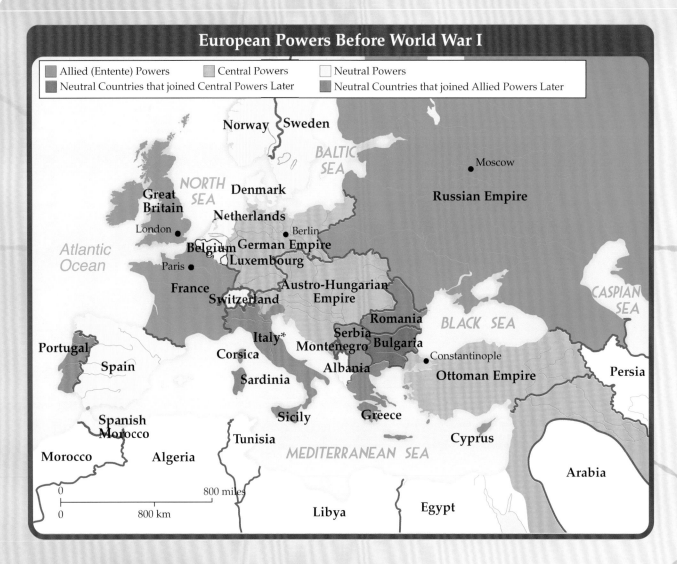

Legend:
- Allied (Entente) Powers
- Central Powers
- Neutral Powers
- Neutral Countries that joined Central Powers Later
- Neutral Countries that joined Allied Powers Later

Map labels: Norway, Sweden, BALTIC SEA, Moscow, Russian Empire, NORTH SEA, Denmark, Great Britain, Netherlands, London, Berlin, German Empire, Belgium, Luxembourg, Atlantic Ocean, Paris, France, Austro-Hungarian Empire, Switzerland, Romania, BLACK SEA, CASPIAN SEA, Italy*, Serbia, Montenegro, Bulgaria, Portugal, Corsica, Albania, Constantinople, Persia, Spain, Sardinia, Ottoman Empire, Spanish Morocco, Sicily, Greece, Cyprus, Tunisia, MEDITERRANEAN SEA, Morocco, Algeria, Arabia, Libya, Egypt

0 — 800 miles
0 — 800 km

Allied Powers

Great Britain, France, Russian Empire, Greece, Portugal, Italy, Serbia, United States, Romania

* Italy joined in 1915

* Portugal and Romania joined in 1916

* Greece and the U.S.A. joined in 1917

Central Powers

German Empire, Ottoman Empire, Austro-Hungarian Empire, Bulgaria

* Italy was aligned with Germany in 1914 but joined the war on the Allied side in 1915

* Bulgaria joined in 1915

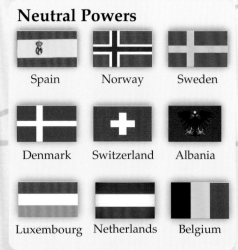

Neutral Powers

Spain, Norway, Sweden, Denmark, Switzerland, Albania, Luxembourg, Netherlands, Belgium

* Luxembourg & Belgium were invaded by Germany in 1940 and were occupied during the full length of the war.

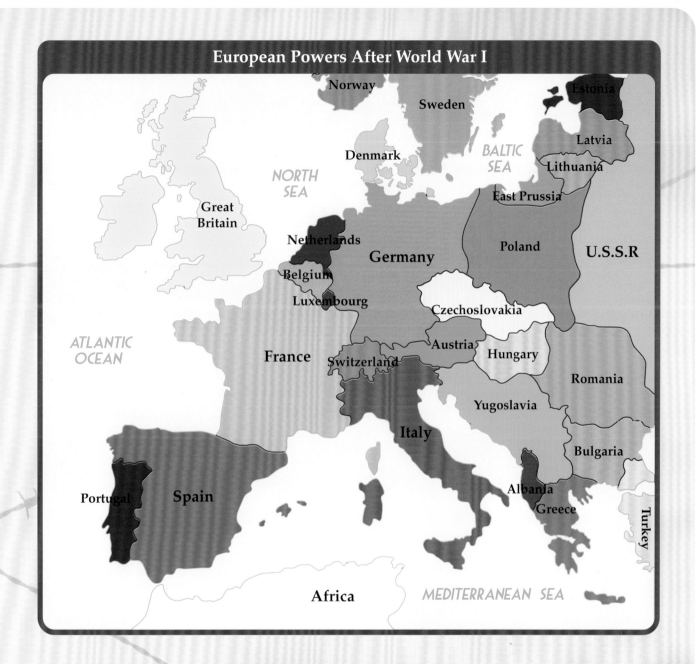

EUROPEAN POWERS AFTER WORLD WAR I

The map of Europe after the war was quite different than it was before the war. The four empires were gone. The U.S.S.R., or United Soviet Socialist Republic, replaced the Russian Empire. While Great Britain and France remained the same, Germany was made smaller.

CHAPTER 1

CANADA ENTERS WORLD WAR I

In 1914, the **Dominion** of Canada was still connected to Britain. Canada governed itself and made its own laws. Newfoundland was not a province of Canada at that time, but a British **colony**.

Major Events
1914

June 28
A Bosnian-Serb assassinates Archduke Franz Ferdinand of Austria-Hungary.

August 5
Canada declares war on Germany.

October
First Canadian soldiers arrive in England.

BELOW: *Posters encouraged Canadians to give money to support the war effort.*

DECLARATION OF WAR

Britain's declaration of war on Germany, on August 4, 1914, meant that Canada was legally at war as well. The Canadian **governor general** declared war between Canada and Germany the following day.

Prime Minister Robert Borden offered Canada's assistance to Great Britain in the war, and the offer was accepted.

Most Canadians supported the war effort. Many volunteered to serve in the war, especially those with strong ties to Britain. Canadian industry changed to manufacture supplies for the war. To raise money to fight the war, the government sold what would later become known as "**Victory Bonds**." These were loans made to the government by citizens.

> It is our duty to let Great Britain know and to let the friends and foes of Great Britain know that there is in Canada but one mind and one heart and that all Canadians are behind the Mother Country.
>
> SIR WILFRED LAURIER, 1914

WHAT DO YOU KNOW?

SUPPORTING THE WAR EFFORT

Montreal businessman Andrew Hamilton Gault used $100,000 of his own money to raise a **militia** regiment to fight in the war. He named it after the governor general's daughter. It was called the Princess Patricia's Canadian Light Infantry, or PPCLI.

ABOVE: *Crowds in London cheered at the news that Britain had declared war on Germany.*

Recruitment and Training

Before 1914, Canada's army had only a few thousand professional soldiers. There was also a large **reserve** force, made up of many local militia units. Canada's Minister of Militia and Defence, Sam Hughes, called for 25,000 new volunteers to come together at Valcartier, north of Quebec City. His swift action turned an empty field at Valcartier into a tent city and training camp – large enough to hold the 33,000 recruits who answered

the call. The army, called the Canadian Expeditionary Force, was suddenly stronger by more than 30,000 soldiers. However, the expanded force lacked proper leadership. After successfully pulling the CEF together so quickly, Hughes assigned positions of command to his friends, even though most of them had little military knowledge or skill. As a result, very little training was accomplished before Canadian forces were sent overseas to England.

BELOW: *Training camps were established in Canada for new recruits to learn skills they would need at the front.*

The Canadian Expeditionary Force

The first group of over 30,000 Canadians arrived in Plymouth, England, in October 1914. They set up a tent camp on Salisbury Plain, in the south of England. The British were unprepared for the arrival of so many poorly equipped Canadians. Once again, the Canadian army camp was disorganized. Many of the first Canadian volunteers had been born in Britain. As the war went on, the numbers of British-born soldiers from Canada began to even out with the number of Canadian-born soldiers, due largely to the role **conscription** played in the war's later years.

SIR SAM HUGHES (1853–1921)

Sir Sam Hughes was Minister of Militia and Defence in the government of Sir Robert Borden. It was his job to prepare Canadian troops for the war and supply their equipment. Hughes insisted Canadian soldiers use the Ross rifle. The Ross rifle was made in Canada but was considered less reliable than the British Lee Enfield rifle. Not everyone approved of Hughes's decisions about how the soldiers should be outfitted and who should be appointed to **officer** positions. British military leaders were not satisfied with Hughes. He was eventually forced to resign in 1916.

WHAT DO YOU THINK?
What things are needed to outfit and train thousands of new soldiers? Where did those things come from?

BELOW: *In 1915, Canadian soldiers arrive by ship in Plymouth, England, to join the war.*

WHAT DO YOU KNOW?

THE MAKEUP OF AN ARMY

Army: An army during World War I was made up of several hundreds of thousands of people. For most of the war, the Canadian Corps was part of the British 1st Army.

Corps: A corps was a subdivision of an army commanded by a lieutenant general. A corps was divided into divisions.

Division: A division was commanded by a major general. Each division included **infantry**, **artillery**, engineers, and medical staff. There were four divisions in the Canadian Corps.

Brigade: Each division of the Canadian Corps had three brigades. A brigade was led by a brigadier and was comprised of four infantry battalions.

Battalion: A battalion was an infantry unit commanded by a lieutenant colonel.

Company: There were four companies in each battalion. They were commanded by a major or captain.

Platoon: Each company had four platoons, which were commanded by a lieutenant.

Section: Within each platoon were four sections. Each section was led by a non-commissioned officer such as a sergeant.

German and Ukrainian immigrants who were not yet Canadian citizens had to register with the government as "enemy aliens" because they had come from countries now at war with Canada. They were not allowed to enlist in the Canadian army, and a large number were even **interned** in camps during the war. Even though soldiers were badly needed, racism proved an obstacle to Canadians who were citizens, but not white. Japanese-Canadians who tried to enlist in British Columbia were refused and had to travel to Alberta to join the army. Black Canadians found it difficult to enlist because of their race. In 1916, No. 2 Construction Battalion was formed in Pictou, Nova Scotia. This was the first all-Black military unit in Canadian history. It served in France in 1917 and 1918. At first, it was assigned to trench-digging. In addition, over 2,000 Blacks enrolled in regular units.

Even though First Nations people were **exempt** from military service, over 3,500 enlisted to serve in World War I. Roughly the same percentage of the First Nations populations volunteered to serve as did the rest of the Canadian population.

TRENCH WARFARE

When the Allies stopped the **initial** German advance into France and Belgium, the two sides reached a point at which neither could make any progress. Both sides dug trenches to better defend their positions and stay hidden from enemy fire. These trenches could extend for many miles (kilometers).

Armies constructed a trench at the front line. There were also two or three lines of trenches behind the first for support and reserve personnel. Trenches were dug in a zigzag pattern.

BELOW: *German troops wait in the trenches for an attack by Allied troops. Their terrible new weapon, the machine gun, will mow the enemy down by the hundreds.*

That way if enemies entered a trench, they could not fire down the length of it. The areas in front of the trench were often protected with barbed wire. Sometimes gaps were left in the wire on purpose to lead attacking troops into a trap.

The area between the two armies' trenches was called "no man's land." Soldiers killed or injured in no man's land were often left there, as there was no way to safely bring them back. Conditions in the trenches were terrible. Soldiers had to deal with mud, water, rats, and dead bodies while living in the trenches.

WHAT DO YOU THINK?
What were conditions in the trenches like?

WHAT DO YOU KNOW?

THE VICTORIA CROSS
The Victoria Cross is the highest medal given to members of the military of British Commonwealth countries for courage in the face of the enemy. It has been awarded less than 1,400 times since it was established in 1856.

CHAPTER 2

CANADA'S EARLIEST BATTLES

Major Events

1914

October 9–November 22
First Battle of Ypres

December 21
First Canadian troops arrive in France.

1915

March 10
Canadian troops support British troops at Neuve Chapelle.

April 22–May 25
Second Battle of Ypres

July 1–November 18
First Battle of the Somme

> We had no sooner entered the trench than we sank, almost up to our knees, in thick clay, mud, and water.
>
> **PRIVATE ALFRED BAGGS, DESCRIBING HIS FIRST NIGHT AT THE FRONT**

ARRIVAL IN FRANCE

The first Canadian fighting unit to arrive in France was the Princess Patricia's Canadian Light Infantry, or PPCLI. They were experienced soldiers who needed little training. They were assigned to be part of a larger British regiment in 1914. They crossed into France on December 21, 1914. There, they served with the British 80th Brigade.

After four months of training, members of the Canadian 1st Division crossed the English Channel to St. Nazaire, France, in February 1915. They were first sent to Fleurbaix, on the French-Belgian border. There they were assigned to support the British Expeditionary Force.

The British troops taught the Canadians how to live in the trenches under enemy fire. The Canadians learned how to deal with artillery and **sniper** fire. They also had to deal with the rats and mud that were part of life on the front. There was little all-out fighting at this location. Still, some Canadians died from sniper fire and **shrapnel** from overhead artillery fire.

LEFT: *Princess Patricia's Canadian Light Infantry parades its colors on their flag in 1915.*

NEUVE CHAPELLE

The Canadians were moved to the battlefront in March 1915. They would support a British-led assault on the town of Neuve Chapelle in northern France on March 10. Since they were new to the **front**, the Canadians were assigned to the very left side of the trenches. Their role was to stay in the trenches. They fired rapidly at the German line as a distraction. The British soldiers moved forward to capture the town of Neuve Chapelle, while the Canadians fired as quickly as possible.

For three hours we fired as rapidly as we could force clips of ammunition into the **magazine** *and for days my shoulder was sore from the recoil of the rifle.*

—A private in the Canadian Infantry

The British were able to capture the town. In fact, they could have advanced even farther through the German line. They chose to stop, though, because the communication lines between the soldiers attacking and British headquarters were cut. The soldiers out front did not want to go too far and get trapped away from the trenches. Still, the operation was a success.

WHAT DO YOU THINK?
How were the first Canadian units used in the larger Allied forces?

Trench Raids

The PPCLI at Neuve Chapelle started the practice of trench raids. A small group of men snuck across no man's land to the enemy trenches at night. There, they launched a surprise attack, stole things, or just **harassed** the enemy. These raids taught valuable skills and were excellent for **morale**.

> "Those raids were extremely effective. They did more to unnerve the enemy, I think, than the battles. The Canadians were ideal for raiding because they could improvise. The Germans couldn't carry out a raid unless they had everything organized. And if anything went wrong with the organization, why, they panicked.
>
> **R.L. CHRISTOPHERSON**
> **5TH WESTERN CAVALRY BATTALION**"

THE SECOND BATTLE OF YPRES

Now the Canadians had some experience. They were ordered to move to the town of Ypres in western Belgium in early April 1915. British and Canadian soldiers called Ypres "Wipers."

The First Battle of Ypres took place in the fall of 1914. Many dead British and German soldiers had been left on the battlefield. As the weather warmed up, the bodies began to rot. A partial British advance in 1914 had produced a **salient**, or bulge, in the front line. This meant that the Germans could fire on the advanced British position from the sides and behind. The Canadians were positioned along this 2-mile-long (3.2 km) salient. The trenches the Canadians took over were poorly built and poorly defended. Ypres was located on a flat plain with **ridges** surrounding the city to the east. The Germans controlled these ridges. They could watch enemy advances from the high ground. French colonial soldiers from Morocco and Algeria were stationed to the west of the Canadians. The British were located to the east.

The Germans began shelling the town of Ypres on Thursday, April 22, 1915. The Allied soldiers knew an attack would follow. That evening, the Germans opened more than 5,500 gas cylinders. The wind carried the gas toward the French and Canadian positions. Most of the gas hit the French colonial troops from Algeria. Faced with this new, horrific weapon, they fled. This created an enormous hole in the defenses to the left of the Canadians.

WHAT DO YOU KNOW?

GAS WARFARE

The use of poisons and gases in warfare was outlawed by the Hague Convention in 1899. Germany, Britain, France, Russia, and the major powers in the war had all signed the treaty. Germany, however, used chlorine gas for the first time at Ypres. Chlorine gas causes temporary blindness and damages the lungs. The victim may suffocate to death. The Allies complained about the German use of gas, but they quickly began developing their own gas weapons.

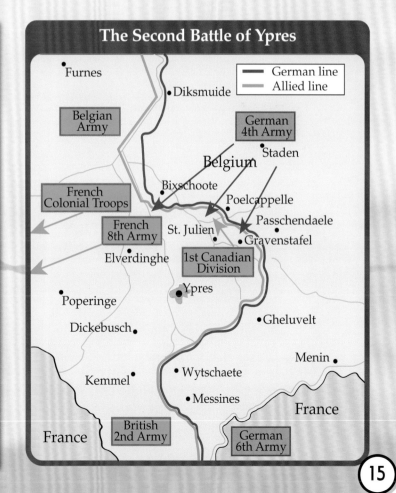

The Second Battle of Ypres

German line
Allied line

Furnes
Diksmuide
Belgian Army
German 4th Army
Staden
Belgium
Bixschoote
French Colonial Troops
Poelcappelle
Passchendaele
French 8th Army
St. Julien
Gravenstafel
Elverdinghe
1st Canadian Division
Ypres
Poperinge
Gheluvelt
Dickebusch
Menin
Kemmel
Wytschaete
Messines
France
British 2nd Army
German 6th Army
France

The Canadians were ordered to close as much of the gap as possible. The Germans started their advance at the same time. At that point, the gas had begun to **disperse**. The Germans expected to move quickly and without **opposition**. The Canadians moved into the empty French positions and fired at the advancing Germans from the side.

The Canadian artillery saw the fighting ahead. They directed fire into the German positions to help. The Canadian cannons became a target for the Germans. Canadian machine gunners set up in front of the cannons. They kept the Germans back while the artillery withdrew.

The 13th Battalion, led by Montreal's Guy Drummond, was eventually overwhelmed by the larger German force. It did, however, push the Germans further north. It also delayed the German advance so that Canadian **reinforcements** could arrive. This prevented the salient from being cut off.

The Canadian troops in reserve were ordered to close the gap. They engaged in heavy fighting immediately. The Canadians kept the Germans from capturing the town of St. Julien, which sat between the front lines and the town of Ypres. The Germans moved into Kitcheners' Wood, just west of St. Julien, to regroup for the night.

FREDERICK FISHER VC (1895–1915)

One of the Canadian machine gunners who set up in front of the Canadian artillery was Lance-Corporal Frederick Fisher of St. Catharines, Ontario. Fisher and his crew ran toward the German position and kept firing until the cannons could be hauled to a safe location. He then set up another position in front of the enemy and kept firing to allow others to escape to safety.

LEFT: *William Nicholson painted five Canadian generals and a major in front of a mural of the destroyed cathedral at Ypres.*

Battle of Kitcheners' Wood

The Canadians needed to do something to further delay the German advance. As the Germans regrouped in Kitcheners' Wood that night, two Canadian reserve battalions were ordered to prepare for a bayonet attack. This would be the first action of the war for these battalions. Shortly before midnight, the Canadians formed eight lines and moved quietly toward the German position for a surprise attack. They made it most of the way before being discovered. At that point, they began a full charge. Several hours of brutal hand-to-hand fighting followed. At the same time, the Canadians were under machine gun fire.

The Canadians captured most of Kitcheners' Wood. The price was very high, though. Over two-thirds of the Canadians attacking the Wood were killed or wounded. This was the first time a Canadian force had defeated a major European power on a European battlefield. At dawn, the Canadian forces could see that the captured position were too vulnerable. The Canadians withdrew to a more heavily defended position south of the Wood.

JOHN MCCRAE (1872–1918)

Lieutenant Colonel John McCrae was a Canadian medical officer. His close friend Alexis Helmer was killed on May 2 during the battle of Ypres. After burying his friend, he noticed the poppies that grew around the war graves in the area. The scene later inspired him to write the famous poem "In Flanders Fields."

BELOW: *The Canadians attack Kitcheners Wood on April 22–23, 1915. It was the first Canadian offensive operation of the war. They recaptured from the Germans the British field guns stolen earlier in the battle.*

Mauser Ridge and the Following Days

The next morning, the Canadians were ordered to capture Mauser Ridge. The Germans were expected to launch an attack there. The Canadian attack was unsuccessful. The field the Canadians had to cross was flat and too exposed to enemy fire.

The Canadians and Germans fought back and forth over the next three days. On April 24, the Germans again used chlorine gas in an attack on the Canadian positions. A Canadian medical officer told the troops to pee on a cloth and hold it over their noses and mouths to **neutralize** the impact of the gas. This saved many lives. It also allowed the Canadians to surprise the German soldiers, who were walking behind the gas cloud.

Canadian Brigadier-General Arthur Currie made a personal appeal to the British commanders for reinforcements. The Canadians had to wait until April 25 to be relieved from the front lines. By that point, many of the soldiers had not slept for several days. They were also suffering from the gas attack. Nearly 6,000 Canadians were lost during the Second Battle of Ypres.

WHAT DO YOU THINK?
What did soldiers do to protect against gas attacks?

BELOW: *During the Second Battle of Ypres, the Germans used chlorine gas for the first time. The Canadians held their part of the Allied front line.*

LEFT: *A British Royal Flying Corps mechanic hands photographic film to an observer in the plane. The observer will fly over German lines gathering information on the enemy.*

CANADIAN PILOTS

At the beginning of the war, the Canadian military tried to create an air force, called the Canadian Air Corps. It was unsuccessful. Canadians who wanted to fly joined the British Royal Flying Corps (RFC) or the Royal Naval Air Service (RNAS) which were combined together in 1918 into the Royal Air Force (RAF). Almost a quarter of the pilots in the RAF during the war were Canadians.

Military pilots flew over enemy territory to get information about where troops were. They also served as spotters to help aim artillery fire. Aircraft were used to drop supplies for friendly troops and drop bombs on the enemy.

Later, new fighter aircraft fought other planes for control of the skies. To be considered an "ace," a fighter pilot had to shoot down five or more enemy aircraft. The top fighter pilot of World War I was German pilot Manfred von Richthofen, known as "The Red Baron." Canadian pilot Roy Brown is **credited** with shooting down the Red Baron. A total of 171 Canadian pilots became aces during World War I.

> I have often been asked what one's sensations were in aerial combat. The answer is it was so exciting that really one's only emotion was excitement.
>
> **FIGHTER PILOT ARCHIBALD JAMES**

FIRST BATTLE OF THE SOMME

The Allies planned an offensive on German-held positions at the Somme, in France, to break through the lines and reduce German numbers. However, the Germans attacked the town of Verdun in early 1916. The French wanted the attack at the Somme moved forward to draw German forces away from Verdun. The First Battle of the Somme began on July 1. The British shelled German trenches, then advanced through the lines. They began with a week-long artillery **barrage** and charged against the Germans who were protected deep in their tunnels.

On the first day of the battle, the 1st Newfoundland Regiment was ordered to charge the German position near the village of Beaumont-Hamel. The regiment was almost completely wiped out. On that day, about 60,000 soldiers under British command were killed, wounded, or missing.

ABOVE: *Members of the 1st Newfoundland Regiment pose before the Battle of Beaumont-Hamel. Only 68 of the regiment's 778 survived.*

WHAT DO YOU KNOW?

1ST NEWFOUNDLAND REGIMENT

At the outbreak of the war, Newfoundland was a dominion of the British Empire. It was not part of Canada. There were enough volunteers from Newfoundland to create a battalion. This became the 1st Newfoundland Regiment. They were known as the "Blue Puttees." They used blue cloth to wrap around their shins, rather than the regular olive color. They served under Britain at Gallipoli before joining the Canadians at the

The months of July and August saw heavy artillery fire and small advances in both directions, but no real progress.

At the end of August 1916, the Canadian Corps moved from Ypres to the Somme. The Canadians took up positions on the front line in September, supporting the Australians. The destruction of the area of the Somme was even more severe than at Ypres. The excellent German defensive trench system against the larger Allied numbers created a **stalemate** on the front.

British General Hubert Gough commanded the Allied reserves, including the Canadians. Gough was impatient and often attacked before it was wise to do so. Gough often sent men into uncut barbed wire, resulting in large numbers of casualties among his men.

By the time the rain began to pick up in late September, the continuous shelling had shattered the chalky ground. When mixed with the rain, the mud became heavy. It stuck to clothes, equipment, and rifles. It made even walking difficult.

FRANCIS PEGAHMAGABOW (1891–1952)

Cpl. Francis "Peggy" Pegahmagabow was Canada's top sniper during World War I. He had more confirmed kills than any other Canadian. He was an Ojibwa from Ontario. He signed up for military service at the outbreak of the war. He served as a scout, messenger, and sniper. He was involved in the battles at Ypres, the Somme, Passchendaele, and Amiens.

BELOW: *On the western front, Allies needed to use hand-to-hand fighting to take trenches from the enemy.*

The Somme was one of the bloodiest battles in the history of warfare. Over 1.2 million men were killed or wounded from both sides. The war had become a "war of **attrition**." This meant that both sides would keep losing soldiers until one side couldn't effectively function any more. The Allies had more men than the Central Powers and could possibly win a war of attrition. This was not good for the men in the field on either side, though.

Flers-Courcelette and Thiepval Ridge

The goal of the Battle of Flers-Courcelette was to punch through the German lines. Then, troops on horseback could drive through and surround the German front. The advance began on September 15, 1916.

Allied troops advanced behind a wall of artillery fire. The artillery was timed to move forward just ahead of the soldiers. This was the first time the Canadians fought together at the division level. The breakthrough never came but, over the next week, the Canadians managed to move the Allied front forward about 1.2 miles (2 km).

The following day, the Canadians attacked the heavily reinforced Thiepval Ridge. This was the first large attack by the Canadian Corps under Sir Hubert Gough. The Allies bombed the enemy from the air. After two days of fighting, the Allies captured the ridge on September 28. The success of the Allied air force pushed the Central Powers to improve their own air force.

BELOW: *The Battle of Flers-Courcelette, September 1916, was fiercely fought by both the Allies and the Germans.*

ABOVE: *The Hour has Struck starting the Battle of the Somme! The Allied first line of attack take up a position in front of their barbed-wire defenses, July 1, 1916, ready to walk across no man's land to attack the German trenches.*

Regina Trench

The German positions were well defended. It took the Allies a month and a half to capture the next trench, Regina Trench, even though they had to advance only about 650 yards (594 m). There were four attempts to capture Regina Trench. The first two failed because the barbed wire protecting the trench was not cut. The Regina Trench was captured by divisions from British Columbia and Saskatchewan in a fourth attack on November 11, 1916.

The Battle of the Somme ended on November 18, 1916. It was one of the deadliest battles in history. Canada's reputation as an effective fighting force had grown. When new offensives began in the spring, Canadian troops would make important contributions.

WHAT DO YOU KNOW?

TANKS

Tanks were developed in part to break the stalemate of trench warfare. Tanks were used as weapons to cross no man's land and break through enemy lines. Early tanks were able to cross trenches and drive over barbed wire. Unfortunately, they were slow and broke down often.

CHAPTER 3

CANADA IN THE LAST TWO YEARS

During the winter, the Allies prepared for a new offensive in the spring. They chose to focus on the Arras region. The Canadian troops would take part.

THE ARRAS OFFENSIVE

The Canadians moved into the Arras region of France to prepare for a spring assault. The Germans had stopped three previous attempts by French and British forces to take back the German-held position of Vimy Ridge. The four Canadian divisions were brought under the same command for the first time in the war. Their commander was British General Julian Byng. Next in command was Canadian General Arthur Currie. Currie spent the winter touring French and British units to learn as much as possible about improving fighting techniques. The Canadians spent the winter preparing for the attack with full-scale rehearsals. Higher ranking officers pretended to be killed so that junior officers learned how to take over during an assault. Soldiers were also trained how to use German machine guns and other artillery in case they needed to use captured weapons to hold off a **counterattack** after attaining the ridge. For the first time, all ranks received maps and plans.

Major Events
1917
April 9–May 16
The Arras Offensive

April 9–April 12
Assault on Vimy Ridge

July 31–November 6
Third Battle of Ypres; Passchendaele Offensive

August 8–12
Battle of Amiens

1918
August 26–September 3
Battle of Arras

September 27–October 11
Battle of Canal du Nord

WHAT DO YOU KNOW?

MINING AND TUNNELING WARFARE

Another way to cross no man's land between the trenches was to dig tunnels. Specialty mining crews dug tunnels all the way under the enemy trench, then set off explosives. Troops could then charge across no man's land while the enemy was distracted.

The artillery, under Lieutenant Colonel Andrew McNaughton, practiced the accuracy and timing of their firing to better support the infantry advance. A vast network of tunnels was dug underground to carry men and **ammunition** to the front. Troops could also use them to bring the wounded and information to the back lines.

General Sir Arthur Currie

General Sir Arthur Currie was born in Ontario and later moved to British Columbia. He was a teacher and, later, a businessman. He joined the militia and rose to command the 5th Regiment (Canadian Garrison Artillery). When World War I broke out, he was offered command of the 2nd Brigade in the Canadian Expeditionary Force. Currie became known for planning and for changing **tactics** to suit the operation at hand. He drew from the experiences of all ranks from Canada and other countries. He always worked to improve tactics and reduce lives lost.

Currie soon gained a reputation as one of Canada's best battlefield commanders. He was given command of the Canadian Corps on June 9, 1917. Following the war, Currie was appointed Inspector General of the Canadian Army. He later became the principal and Vice Chancellor of McGill University in Montreal.

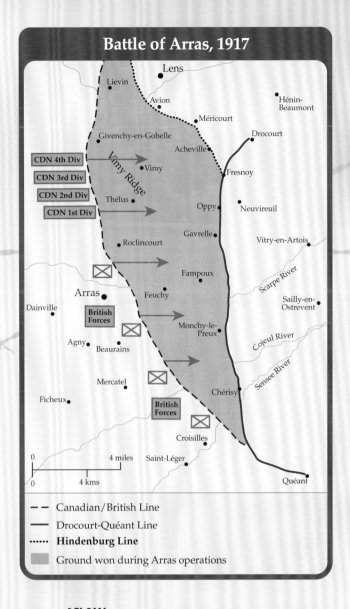

Battle of Arras, 1917

Lens
Lievin
Avion
Hénin-Beaumont
Méricourt
Givenchy-en-Gohelle
Drocourt
Acheville
CDN 4th Div
Vimy Ridge
Vimy
Fresnoy
CDN 3rd Div
CDN 2nd Div
Thélus
Oppy
Neuvireuil
CDN 1st Div
Gavrelle
Vitry-en-Artois
Roclincourt
Fampoux
Scarpe River
Arras
Feuchy
Sailly-en-Ostrevent
Dainville
British Forces
Monchy-le-Preux
Cojeul River
Agny
Beaurains
Sensee River
Mercatel
Chérisy
Ficheux
British Forces
Croisilles
0   4 miles   Saint-Léger
0   4 kms
Quéant

- - - Canadian/British Line
——— Drocourt-Quéant Line
······ **Hindenburg Line**
▨ Ground won during Arras operations

BELOW: *Major-General Arthur Currie, commander of the Canadian Corps*

LEFT: *A tank leads Canadian troops to the German trenches, past a fallen Canadian soldier at Vimy Ridge on Easter Monday in April 1917.*

VIMY RIDGE

Taking Vimy Ridge was an important strategic objective for the Allies. If they could take the ridge, they would have a good view of the surrounding area and be able to see German positions.

April 9

In advance of the attack, Allied artillery fired for two weeks. This damaged German positions and prevented the German resupply lines from operating.

The Canadian attack began at 5:30 a.m. on Monday, April 9, 1917, in a storm of sleet. As practiced, the Canadian artillery used its new "rolling barrage" tactic. Artillery fire led the advance, moving ahead at the same pace as the soldiers walking across the battlefield. This helped provide soldiers with better cover. Then artillery units also timed their advances, with some guns moving while others were firing. They never paused for the Germans to counterattack. The advance went well. The Canadians captured the German front line very quickly.

WHAT DO YOU KNOW?

HEROES OF VIMY

The Canadian advance was slowed by nests of German machine gunners. Lance-Sergeant Ellis Sifton, Private William Milne, and Captain Thain MacDowell each crawled under machine-gun fire to different nests and eliminated them. Each was awarded the Victoria Cross for his actions.

> We felt so safe with that rolling barrage in front. You could see the thing beating. It was like a lawnmower, you know, when you're cutting grass.
>
> **H. CAMPBELL, 14TH BATTALION CANADIAN EXPEDITIONARY FORCE**

April 10

The attack was going well, but the troops were very tired. A new wave of Canadian soldiers entered the battle the next day. By 11:00 a.m., the front line had reached the next **checkpoint**. The troops took a planned pause to make sure the area behind was secure. At the same time, the artillery bombed the area ahead. Machine guns and other weapons were carried forward for use in the next advance. Two main targets remained: Hill 145 and "the Pimple." The Pimple was a heavily protected point at the top of the highest hill in the area.

The Canadians needed to secure as much territory as possible before nightfall. Hill 145 was a particularly important **objective**. At about 6:00 p.m., an inexperienced group of soldiers from the 85th Battalion (Nova Scotia Highlanders) walked straight up Hill 145. They did not even have artillery support. They overtook the Germans in a brief but difficult fight. The Germans on Hill 145 never expected such a direct, unprotected attack.

> " Under the orders of your devoted officers in the coming battle you will advance or fall where you stand facing the enemy. To those who will fall I say, 'You will not die, but step into immortality. Your mothers will not lament your fate, but will be proud to have borne such sons. Your name will be revered forever and ever by your grateful country, and God will take you unto Himself.'
>
> **SIR ARTHUR CURRIE, COMMANDER, CANADIAN CORPS, SPECIAL ORDER BEFORE VIMY RIDGE** "

RIGHT: *At Vimy Ridge, Canadian machine gunners set up their guns in shell holes waiting for the inevitable counterattack.*

ABOVE: *Throughout the Battle of Vimy Ridge, the Canadian artillery kept up a constant barrage on the German trenches.*

April 11–12

The Canadians expected counterattacks the following days, but none happened. On April 12, the Canadians moved on the last major fortification on Vimy Ridge: the Pimple. The Canadians advanced quietly through blowing snow in the very early morning and attacked. The battle did not last long. The Canadians captured the location and pressed on.

The Canadians had captured Vimy Ridge, suffering over 10,000 casualties in the battle. Vimy Ridge remained under Allied control for the rest of the war.

The capture of Vimy Ridge was a source of great pride and confidence for the Canadians. French and British armies had tried for three years to secure the ridge. The successful battle helped Canada to be viewed differently by the world, not just as a dominion of Britain.

I have always felt that Canadian nationality was born on the top of Vimy Ridge...There was a feeling that we had mastered the job and that we were the finest troops on earth. This is where Canadian nationality first came together, when all of us were fused or welded, if you like, into a unity.

—E. S. Russenholt, 44th (Manitoba) Battalion

Billy Bishop William Avery "Billy" Bishop was born in Owen Sound, Ontario in 1894. He entered the Royal Military College of Canada in 1911. When the war broke out, he joined a **cavalry** regiment and was sent overseas to England and then France. As there was no Canadian air force, he joined the Royal Flying Corps as an observer. For his job, he took pictures of enemy troops from the air. Bishop trained as a fighter pilot in 1916 and transferred to France the following year. He soon showed success shooting down enemy aircraft and quickly became an ace.

Bishop developed new methods for aerial combat and became the most successful Canadian pilot of the war. During the battle of Vimy Ridge, he shot down 12 aircraft and was then promoted to captain. Bishop was later awarded a Victoria Cross for his solo raid on a German airfield. In 1918, he was sent back to England to establish the new Canadian Flying Corps. He later became air marshal of the Royal Canadian Air Force.

BELOW: *Canadian "ace" Billy Bishop is credited with shooting down 72 German planes during World War 1, the most of any Allied fighter pilot.*

WHAT DO YOU THINK?
How would aircraft be used during the war?

"[The Canadian Corps is] the ram with which we will break up the last resistance of the German army.

MARSHAL FOCH, COMMANDER-IN-CHIEF OF THE ALLIED ARMIES"

HILL 70

General Byng was promoted after the Arras Offensive. Brigadier-General Currie took over as commander of the Canadian Corps. His first assignment was to capture the coal mining town of Lens, France, near the Belgian border. The hill overlooking Lens was more important strategically than the town itself. Currie made Hill 70 the main goal.

The Allied generals decided to use a **diversion** before attacking the hill directly. The generals told the Canadian Corps to attack the German trenches east of Hill 70.

The 116th Battalion was chosen to make the diversionary raid on the night of July 23. Canadian artillery started the attack. Their shells cut a path through the German barbed wire. Then the Canadian soldiers charged across no man's land.

The German troops lived in dugouts deep in the earth. There, the men were protected from the artillery fire. The Canadians threw bombs into the dugouts to kill the German troops. The Germans came running out of the dugouts to force the Canadians back. Many soldiers were killed and wounded on both sides.

In the darkness, it became difficult to tell friend from foe. Many Canadian officers and sergeants were killed or wounded. Without their leaders, some soldiers could not figure out how to get back to the Canadian trenches.

Lieutenant Maurice Crabtree from C Company took command and issued orders to the Canadian troops. He told them how to get back to the Canadian lines. He also set up a rear guard group. They would fight off the Germans while the rest of the Canadian troops retreated.

LEFT: *After the raid, Lieutenant Crabtree was awarded the Military Cross for bravery and taking command of a dangerous situation. King George V presented him with the award at Buckingham Palace.*

BELOW: *A German soldier emerges from a deep dugout to surrender to Allied soldiers. This is the type of dugout that Lt. Crabtree and the 116th batallion were attempting to destroy on their night raid.*

MUSTARD GAS

Mustard gas caused severe blisters on the skin of the soldiers who came into contact with it. It stuck to the ground and remained dangerous for a long time. In some cases, an area was doused with mustard gas to prevent enemy soldiers from even entering it.

BELOW: *An officer rallies his men as they advance on Hill 70.*

SIR JULIAN BYNG
(1862–1935)

British General Sir Julian Byng was appointed to command the Canadian Corps from May 1916 to June 1917. Byng helped make the Canadian Corps into a professional fighting army. Byng and Currie both believed in thorough preparation and changing tactics to suit the task. Byng's nickname was "Bungo," and he got along well with all ranks he commanded. The Canadians called themselves "Byng Boys," taking pride in his leadership. When Byng was promoted to lead the British Third Army, he recommended that Currie be given command of the Canadians. After the war, General Byng was appointed the governor general of Canada from 1921 to 1926.

Canadians Take the Hill

Meanwhile, the direct attack by Canadian forces on Hill 70 began in the early morning hours of August 15, 1917. They used similar tactics as the attack on Vimy Ridge. The assault progressed well. The Germans began using mustard gas against the Canadians. The Germans also used flamethrowers to try to cut the Canadian lines.

During one of the German counterattacks, Major Okill Massey Learmonth, from Quebec City, directed the defense of the area.

Learmonth actually caught German **grenades** that were thrown at his men and threw them back. He continued to fight even when severely wounded. He was later awarded the Victoria Cross.

The Canadians captured Hill 70 ten days after the battle began. Afterward, a quiet period allowed them to prepare to move on to Passchendaele.

PASSCHENDAELE AND THE THIRD BATTLE OF YPRES

British forces began a major offensive in the second half of 1917. Their goal was to take back German-held ports in Belgium. Ypres and the nearby village of Passchendaele would be a major focus of this campaign. The towns were in the small area of Belgium still under Allied control. They were located close to an important railway line that brought supplies to the German soldiers. The attack at Passchendaele began on July 31, 1917. The first advance was successful for the first couple of miles. Then the Allies ran into a new enemy: rain. The low-lying plain around Passchendaele soon became a huge vat of waist-deep mud, littered with thousands of dead bodies.

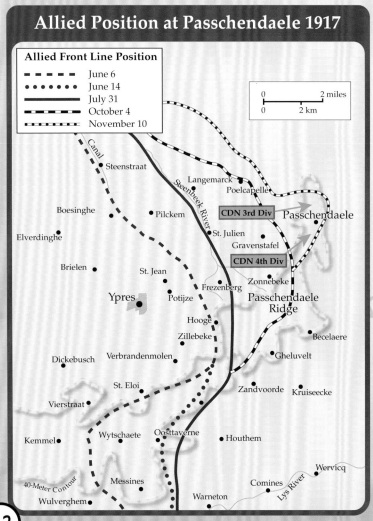

Allied Position at Passchendaele 1917

Allied Front Line Position
- – – – June 6
- • • • • June 14
- ——— July 31
- –■–■– October 4
- ■·■·■· November 10

0   2 miles
0   2 km

Steenstraat
Langemarck
Poelcapelle
Boesinghe
Pilckem
CDN 3rd Div
Passchendaele
Elverdinghe
St. Julien
Gravenstafel
CDN 4th Div
Brielen
St. Jean
Zonnebeke
Ypres
Potijze
Frezenberg
Passchendaele Ridge
Hooge
Zillebeke
Becelaere
Dickebusch
Verbrandenmolen
Gheluvelt
St. Eloi
Zandvoorde
Kruiseecke
Vierstraat
Wytschaete
Oosttaverne
Houthem
Kemmel
Wervicq
40-Meter Contour
Messines
Comines
Lys River
Wulverghem
Warneton

ABOVE: *At Passchendaele, Canadian machine gunners used shell holes as protection as they stopped German counterattacks with their machine guns.*

The Germans held all of the surrounding ridges, and the Allies held the low, flat plain that extended into the middle. This meant that the Allied troops in the salient could be fired on from three sides. The Germans could watch their movements from the high ground. The most prominent of the ridges around the Ypres salient was Passchendaele Ridge. The German defenses included square, reinforced concrete buildings called **pillboxes**, with walls and roofs that were 5 feet (1.5 m) thick. These pillboxes provided soldiers with shelter during artillery bombardments.

The Canadians were ordered to capture Passchendaele Ridge in mid-October 1917. They began planning an attack, drawing on the successes at Vimy. They also took into account the conditions at Passchendaele. The attack began on the morning of October 26, 1917.

Just like at Vimy, the Canadians advanced on Passchendaele Ridge behind a wall of carefully timed artillery fire. It was much harder to keep up because of the mud, and many soldiers fell behind. Many individual feats of bravery and daring allowed the Canadians to hold positions in the face of German counterattacks.

WHAT DO YOU KNOW?

THE MUDDY FIELD AT PASSCHENDAELE

Heavy rains in October turned the battlefield around Passchendaele into a great muddy swamp. Movement through the mud became difficult and dangerous. The only way across the deep mud was on wooden tracks, called duckboards. The Germans were aware of this and often shelled the duckboard tracks. This would cut off resupply routes until the boards could be replaced.

> "For most conspicuous bravery and resource when the right **flank** of our attack was held up by heavy machine-gun and rifle fire from a 'pill-box' strong point. Heavy casualties were producing a critical situation when Pte. Holmes, on his own initiative and single-handed, ran forward and threw two bombs, killing and wounding the crews of two machine guns. He then returned to his comrades, secured another bomb, and again rushed forward alone under heavy fire and threw the bomb into the entrance of the 'pill-box,' causing the nineteen occupants to surrender. By this act of valor at a very critical moment, Pte. Holmes undoubtedly cleared the way for the advance of our troops and saved the lives of many of his comrades.
>
> WRITTEN OF PRIVATE THOMAS HOLMES, VC, LONDON GAZETTE, NO. 30471, 11 JANUARY, 1918"

The second advance came on October 30. Fresh soldiers replaced those who had been at the front for the first attack. Again the advance was small. They gained only about 550 yards (503 m). In the next few days, the Canadians **consolidated** their positions and slowly rotated people away from the front line. The 1st and 2nd Divisions took their places.

The third phase of the attack began on November 6, 1917. By now, the ground had begun to dry. The fresh soldiers made a rapid charge up the two sides of the ridge in the early morning hours and captured it. They then moved on and took the town of Passchendaele after much hand-to-hand fighting. The last German position in the area was a hill to the east of the village. By November 10, the Canadians had secured that as well. In the two weeks of battle, the Canadians had lost more than 5,000 men. They had again captured a ridge that most thought was impossible to win.

WHAT DO YOU KNOW?

CONSCRIPTION CRISIS OF 1917

After the massive losses of personnel during the Battle of the Somme, Canada required more men to serve in the army as soldiers. There were not enough volunteers to meet the need. The government of Sir Robert Borden turned to conscription. The idea of being forced to fight in the war was very unpopular in Quebec. Quebeckers at the time felt no ties with either Britain or France. Borden won the 1917 election, but he had almost no support from Quebec. He brought conscription to Canada in 1918, which was met with violent protests in Quebec.

THE HUNDRED DAYS OFFENSIVE

Collapsing under a revolution against its monarchy at home, Russia withdrew from the war in 1917. This allowed the Germans to move troops from the Eastern to the Western Front. In March 1918, the Germans made a large offensive against the British and French troops in northern France. The Canadians were stationed in Arras at this point and were held in reserve during the initial German attack. After a third attack, the Germans had gained a lot of ground. Now, however, their lines were stretched too far. The Germans were unable to break through the Allied lines. When the Germans broke off the offensive at the end of July, the time was right for an Allied counterattack. The Hundred Days Offensive was a push by the Allies against the weakened western part of the German line. The Allies hoped the offensive would drive the Germans out of France. The offensive began on August 8, 1918.

WHAT DO YOU THINK?
Why did countries have to turn to conscription?

Amiens

The first assault of the Hundred Days Offensive took place at Amiens. Earlier raids by Australian troops had determined that the ground in the area was solid enough to use tanks. A combined force of troops from Britain, France, Canada, Australia, and New Zealand attacked the Germans at Amiens on August 8. In addition to the direct attack, Lieutenant Gordon Flowerdew led the Canadian Cavalry Brigade in an attack from the side. The weakened German army could not put up effective resistance.

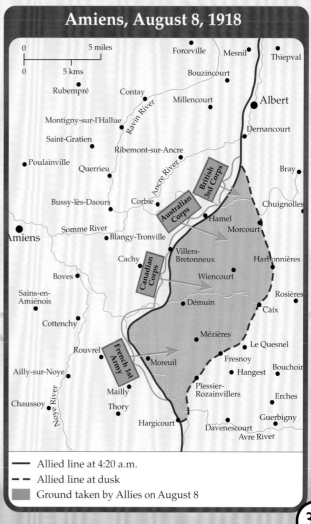

Amiens, August 8, 1918

— Allied line at 4:20 a.m.
-- Allied line at dusk
▨ Ground taken by Allies on August 8

The Allies advanced over 7 miles (11 km) the first day of the attack. This was a huge boost for the Allies, while the impact on German morale was devastating. German General Eric Ludendorff called it "the black day of the German Army." By the second day, the infantry had advanced farther than the artillery could fire. The battle was over by August 12, and the Germans retreated. German losses included over 30,000 people killed or captured. After their breakthrough at Amiens, the Canadians were shifted back to Arras. There, they were given the task of breaking through the **Hindenburg Line**.

ABOVE: *Canadian troops on the way to the front lines step aside on the left to allow German prisoners to get by during the Battle of Amiens.*

> *You know, when you'd been to Ypres and you'd been around the Somme, when you got two hundred yards or a hundred yards, you thought you'd made a wonderful advance. But here, we'd gone miles. It was unbelievable.*
>
> —Samuel Hemphill,
> 10th (Western Canadians) Battalion

Arras

German defenses in the Arras region were well established. They included large trench systems. A break here would allow the Allies to go around a large part of the Hindenburg Line.

The Battle of Arras began on August 26, 1918. The Canadian 3rd Division captured their goals quickly. But the following day they had difficulty getting to the German trenches. On August 28 and 29, the 1st Division relieved the exhausted 2nd Division. The fresh troops broke through the first German trench. They paused to clear the trench instead of moving forward. By September, the Canadians had captured their objectives. They wanted to use this territory as a jumping off point for attacking the Drocourt-Quéant Line. A third offensive began on September 2. The Canadians expected a counterattack the next day, but it never came. The Germans retreated from the Drocourt-Quéant Line. The Canadians had won another major battle.

Canal du Nord / Cambrai

The next position to be taken by the Canadians lay on the other side of a large marshy area. The only passable section was a dry lake bed. It was only about 1.4 miles (2.3 km) wide. Currie's staff members planned the attack with their usual efficiency. A specialty unit of engineers built wooden bridges to cross the canal for the assault. The corps prepared for the crossing in hiding, so the Germans would not expect the attack.

The British army launched a smaller attack at another nearby location. They hoped to draw the Germans from the Canadian Corps' hidden position. On September 27, 1918, the Canadians crossed the canal in the early morning. They broke through the Hindenburg Line. The four Canadian divisions fought 10 German divisions for two weeks. Over 18,000 Canadians were killed, wounded, or missing during the battle. On October 11, 1918, the Canadian forces drove the Germans out of their supply depot at Cambrai.

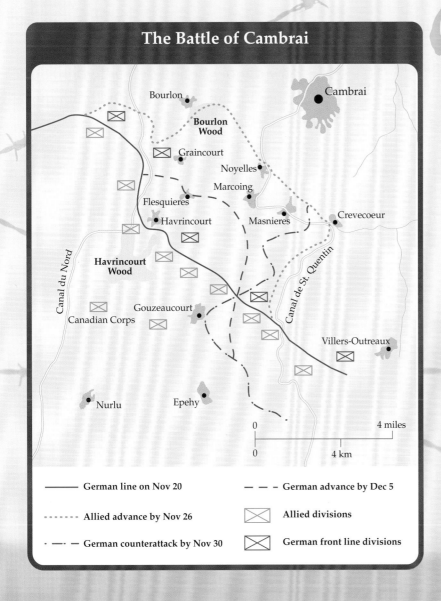

The Battle of Cambrai

Bourlon
Cambrai
Bourlon Wood
Graincourt
Noyelles
Marcoing
Flesquieres
Crevecoeur
Havrincourt
Masnieres
Havrincourt Wood
Gouzeaucourt
Canadian Corps
Villers-Outreaux
Nurlu
Epehy
Canal du Nord
Canal de St. Quentin

0   4 miles
0   4 km

—————— German line on Nov 20

– – – German advance by Dec 5

· · · · · · Allied advance by Nov 26

⊠ Allied divisions

– · – · German counterattack by Nov 30

⊠ German front line divisions

> "The banks of this unfinished part of the Canal were something like twenty feet high, I should think, and we were supposed to have scaling ladders brought up to us the night before. You can imagine my feeling when they didn't arrive. But somehow, they climbed on each other's shoulders and got up.
>
> **C.B. PRICE, 14TH BATTALION CANADIAN EXPEDITIONARY FORCE**

ABOVE: *The first Canadian platoon to enter Valenciennes on their way to the Canal du Nord*

CAPTAIN OULSON NORMAN MITCHELL, VC
(1889–1978)

Captain Mitchell was an engineer from Winnipeg. He served with a tunneling company in the Canadian Expeditionary Force. During the Battle of Cambrai, he was supposed to make sure the bridges would be safe for troops to cross. He **defused** several explosive charges under a bridge while under heavy enemy fire. At another location, he ran across a bridge and again removed the charges while the enemy tried to set them off. He received the Victoria Cross for his efforts.

CHAPTER 4

THE END OF THE WAR

THE FINAL DAYS OF FIGHTING

The Germans were now in full retreat. The Canadians chose to go after them. Over the next few weeks, the Canadian Corps chased the Germans out of France and into Belgium. German morale had collapsed. There was talk that the war would soon be over. Currie had heard talk like that before. He was not convinced it would happen so quickly. His men fought a final battle with the Germans in Mons, Belgium. The Canadians took the town on November 9 and 10.

The First World War ended with an **armistice** that took effect the next day. The Canadian Corps suffered 46,000 casualties during the Hundred Days Offensive. The last Canadian to be killed was George Lawrence Price. He died just minutes before the armistice took effect at 11:00 a.m. on November 11. He is traditionally known as the last soldier killed in World War I.

Major Events

1918

November 10–11
Battle of Mons

November 11
The armistice is signed between Germany and the Allies.

1920
The Group of Seven is founded.

1921
Canadian women get the right to vote.

1926

November 15
The Balfour Declaration

1931

December 11
Statute of Westminster

BELOW: *Canadian troops and Belgian civilians celebrate the signing of the armistice on November 11.*

> I cannot but think we have much to be thankful for, and more still to hope for in the future.
>
> WINSTON CHURCHILL TO DAVID LLOYD GEORGE, DECEMBER 9, 1918

WAR ARTISTS

Sir Max Aitken (Lord Beaverbrook) was a wealthy newspaper owner and businessman from New Brunswick. He established a program to record the events of the war through art. The German gas attack at Ypres was never photographed. Aitken believed there should be a permanent record of such things. He created the Canadian War Memorials Fund, which was used to pay prominent artists to sketch the battles. Later, these artists created paintings based on those sketches. The first artist sponsored was British artist Richard Jack, who created a painting of the Battle of Ypres.

Canadian artists were hired more often as the program took root. Group of Seven artists A. Y. Jackson, Fred Varley, and Arthur Lismer were part of this program. Other major Canadian artists involved include Maurice Cullen and David Milne. Quebec artist, Henrietta Mabel May, was commissioned to do work for the Canadian War Memorial and painted Canadian women working in ammunition factories.

RIGHT: *This painting by Canadian war artist A.Y. Jackson shows Canadian troops trudging through the remains of a small forest destroyed during a battle.*

THE GROUP OF SEVEN

During World War I, a new art movement started in Canada. Members of the movement would become known as the Group of Seven. They met in Toronto between 1911 and 1913. The group got its name when they did a show together in 1920. The group included Franklin Carmichael, Lawren Harris, A. Y. Jackson, Frank Johnston, Arthur Lismer, J. E. H. Macdonald, and F. H. Varley.

The group members wanted Canada to have its own style of art. They were attracted to the Canadian landscape, particularly the rugged areas of northern Ontario. When the group formed, they focused on landscape painting.

The Group of Seven artists created a style unique to Canada. Many of their paintings used simple forms and bright colors. They also focused on communicating their feelings through their art. They often painted together.

The artists were helped by the head of the National Gallery of Canada, Eric Brown. He purchased their paintings and made sure they got lots of press. During the 1920s, people started calling them a national school of painters for Canada. In 1930, they began inviting painters from across the country to join. In 1933, the name changed to the Canadian Group of Painters. Even more artists were brought into the group.

F. H. VARLEY
(1881–1969)

Frederick Varley was born in Sheffield, England, and studied art in England and Belgium. He emigrated to Canada in 1912, and worked as a commercial artist in Toronto. In 1918, Canadian War Records commissioned Varley to serve as a war artist. He quickly gained fame for his moving paintings of the war. In 1920, Varley became a founding member of the Group of Seven. Later he taught art and worked both as a portraitist and landscape artist.

BELOW: *Canadian war artist Fred Varley called his painting "For What?" It shows the dead being buried in no man's land after a battle.*

ABOVE: *This painting by Arthur Lismer shows a Canadian ship painted to break up its outline so that a German U-boat captain might not think it is an Allied warship.*

SOCIETAL CHANGES

Canadian society changed significantly during World War I. The economy benefited by the increased need for Canadian manufacturers to make war supplies for the Allied armies and send foodstuffs and raw materials. The added demand resulted in higher prices at home. The need for extra factory workers, along with soldiers to send overseas, created labor shortages too. Canada transformed from a mostly **rural** economy to a more industrialized nation. In 1917, the Canadian government introduced income taxation, as other countries such as the United States and Great Britain had done before the war. The tax intended as a temporary measure, was never discontinued.

The role of women changed significantly. They began to work in factories, manufacturing, and in other jobs traditionally done by men. Women who had relatives serving in the war were first given the right to vote in 1917. A law giving all women over the age of 21 the right to vote was passed in 1918. Three years later, Agnes Macphail became the first woman elected to the Canadian parliament.

ABOVE: *Canadian women gained the right to vote in 1918.*

CANADA'S LEGACY FROM WORLD WAR I

Canada entered the war as a British dominion. The distinguished service of the Canadian Corps gave Canada a sense of recognition and respect on an international scale that it did not have before. Canadian Prime Minister Sir Robert Borden and other leaders of British dominions were given seats at the peace talks at the end of the war. Canada also gained its own seat in the League of Nations. The League of Nations was created to help promote peace and good relations between its member countries.

Trouble at Home

Many issues arose following the war. People were unhappy with high prices. Worker strikes broke out across Canada, and membership in labor unions rose. Farm workers joined together with the labor unions as well. In 1921, the farm workers' Progressive Party was the second largest political party in Canada's House of Commons. They demanded farm price supports and **regulation** of grain and transportation businesses. An economic downturn caused the movement to lose some strength. Workers lost their jobs, and union membership fell.

Divisions between French and English Canada were brought on by the Conscription Crisis of 1917. These divisions would exist for decades to come. They would also influence Canadian foreign policy. Between World Wars I and II, Canada would become **isolationist**. This meant they did not have dealings with other nations as much. They wanted to stay out of other nations' problems.

An Empire in Decline

The British Empire was slowly changing into the **British Commonwealth**. It gave some former colonies more control over their own governments. In Canada, many Canadians were pushing for greater independence from Britain. This push helped get W. L. Mackenzie King elected as prime minister. King would work with other leaders to loosen ties between Britain and the dominions.

In 1926, a conference of leaders from the British Empire drew up the Balfour Declaration. The Balfour Declaration said that the United Kingdom and all its dominions would have equal status in all areas. They would be united together as equals within the British Commonwealth. Canada and other British dominions now could determine their own foreign policies. Also, British Parliament could not pass laws affecting dominions unless the parliament of the dominion agreed. The 1931 Statute of Westminster confirmed the declaration's proposals. Canada was not an independent country yet, but it had taken an important step toward freeing itself from Britain's control.

LEFT: *A Canadian soldier is honored with the Distinguished Conduct Medal for his bravery on the battlefield.*

WHAT DO YOU THINK?
How did Canada relate to other nations after World War I?

The Great Depression and Back to War

The global economic downturn, known as the **Great Depression**, hit Canada hard. Canada had strong economic ties to the United States. When the U.S. economy collapsed, Canada's economy faltered soon after. In the early 1930s, Canada focused on its economic struggles. The government under Prime Minister King did little to fight the depression. Canada tried to fix its economic problems by increasing trade with other nations.

Canada could keep to itself for only so long. Once again, German, as well as Japanese, aggression would become a danger to the League of Nations. Canada once again had to consider whether to fight in another world war. But this time, Prime Minister King declared, Canada's "parliament will decide."

BELOW: *(front row) King George V posed between British Prime Minister Baldwin (left) and Canadian Prime Minister Mackenzie King (right). In the back row (l to r) are the leaders of Newfoundland, Australia, South Africa, New Zealand, and the Irish Free State.*

W. L. MACKENZIE KING (1874–1950)

Mackenzie King's family had long worked for Canadian independence. In 1908, King was elected to parliament. He became Canada's first full-time labor minister. In 1919, he became the leader of Canada's Liberal Party. He was elected prime minister in 1921. He went to the Imperial Conference in London in 1928. King worked hard to gain equality status for Canada and other self-governing Commonwealth members.

FURTHER READING AND WEBSITES

FURTHER READING

Christie, Norm M. *Gas Attack! The Canadians at Ypres, 1915.* Nepean: CEF Books, 1998.

Christie, Norm M. *Futility & Sacrifice: The Canadians on the Somme, 1916.* Nepean: CEF Books, 1998.

Christie, Norm M. *Winning the Ridge: The Canadians at Vimy, 1917.* Nepean: CEF Books, 1998.

Christie, Norm M. *Slaughter in the Mud: The Canadians at Passchendaele, 1917.* Nepean: CEF Books, 1998.

Cook, Tim. *At the Sharp End: Canadians Fighting in the Great War 1914–1916.* Toronto: Penguin Canada, 2007.

Cook, Tim. *Shock Troops: Canadians Fighting in the Great War 1917–1918.* Toronto: Penguin Canada, 2009.

WEBSITES

The Canadian War Museum
www.warmuseum.ca

Archives Canada
www.collectionscanada.gc.ca/ firstworldwar/index-e.html

Veterans Affairs Canada
www.veterans.gc.ca/eng/ remembrance/history/first-world-war

The Canadian Military History Gateway
www.cmhg.gc.ca

For King and Empire: Canada's Soldiers in the Great War
www.kingandempire.com

The National Film Board of Canada: Images of a Forgotten War
www3.nfb.ca/ww1/

GLOSSARY

ammunition	projectiles used in battle, such as grenades, bullets, or artillery shells
armistice	an agreement to temporarily stop the fighting; truce
artillery	large caliber weapons, such as cannons, that are operated by crews
attrition	a gradual reduction in numbers through death or injury
Balkan	the easternmost of Europe's peninsulas, comprised of modern-day Slovenia, Croatia, Bosnia and Herzegovina, Serbia, Kosovo, Montenegro, Macedonia, Albania, Bulgaria, Romania, and Moldova
barrage	a rapid series of artillery fire
British Commonwealth	an association of countries with links to the United Kingdom
cavalry	soldiers who fight on horseback or in light armored vehicles
checkpoint	a pre-determined location to stop and check that all is well
colony	a territory that is controlled by or belongs to another country
conscription	mandatory enrollment in the armed forces
consolidated	joined together; combined into a single system
counterattack	attack by a defending force against an attacking enemy force in order to regain lost ground
credited	recognized for an achievement
defused	disabled an explosive device by removing the fuse; made less dangerous
disperse	spread in different directions; scatter
diversion	a distraction; something that takes attention away from a particular event
dominion	a territory that is under the control of the British government
exempt	freed from doing something that others are required to do
flank	side
front	the area where military forces are fighting; the most forward line of a combat force
governor general	commander-in-chief in Canada; also serves as the representative of the British monarch in Canada
Great Depression	one of the most severe economic downturns in recent history that started in 1929 and continued during the 1930s

grenades	small bombs that are typically thrown by hand
harass	wear down an enemy by making repeated attacks; torment
Hindenburg Line	German defensive position on the Western Front that was first built during the winter of 1916–1917; eventually it consisted of six heavily fortified defensive lines
infantry	a branch of the military that fights on foot
initial	the first or beginning
interned	to be confined within a certain area, usually by a government during a time of war
isolationist	someone who believes that a country should not be involved or have dealings with other countries
magazine	a device that feeds ammunition into a firearm
militia	a military unit composed of volunteers who normally have other jobs
morale	feelings of enthusiasm or willingness that a person or a group has about a job
nationalism	devotion to the interests or culture of a particular nation
neutralize	make something ineffective; stop from being harmful
objective	a goal or purpose
officer	a military person who holds a position of command or authority
opposition	resistance; actions by a person or group that you are trying to defeat
pillbox	a small reinforced structure built to defend a protected area
regulation	rule or law controlling how something should be done
reinforcements	groups brought in to help those who started an action or activity
reserve	parts of a country's armed forces not on active duty but subject to serving in an emergency
ridges	long narrow hilltops
rural	relating to the country, not a city or urban area
salient	a bulge forward in the front
shrapnel	small pieces that fly out from a bomb, shell, or other explosion
sniper	a soldier who is a skilled long-range shooter
stalemate	a situation in which further action is blocked; a deadlock
tactics	actions or ways to achieve a goal
victory bond	a promise by a government to pay back a loan of money given to it, with interest. These were sold to help the government get the cash required to pay for supplies for the soldiers.

INDEX